FEBRUARY 2022

THE URBAN MARKET

EXECUTIVE YOUTH LEADERS

HALZ SIMONS
&
BELOVED JOSHUA SIMONS

EDUCATION, BUSINESS TIPS, COMMUNITY NEWS

Beloved J & Halz S

Tells Us All About Their Journey From Sport To Business Owners To Leadership In the Community

Is it Possible To BRIDGE THE GAP?

IT'S TIME TO GO DEEP SUMMIT
AN INTERNATIONAL DEVELOPMENT SUMMIT TRANSFORMING QUALITY ASSETS

JANUARY 13 - 15, 2022

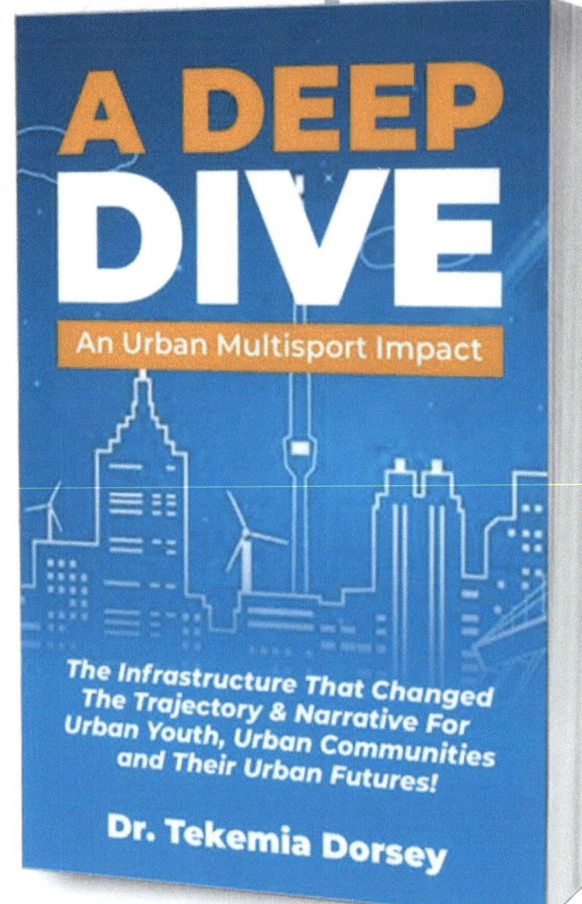
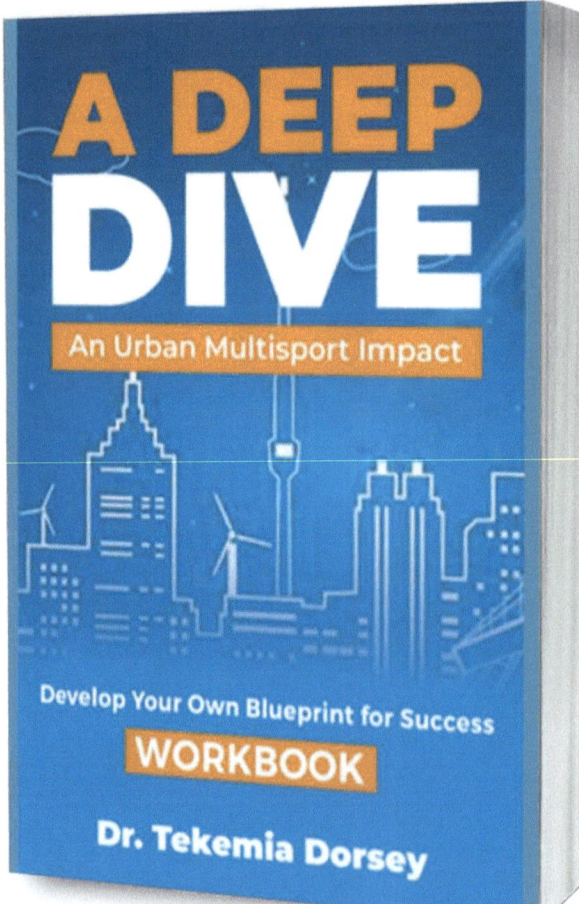

A DEEP DIVE BOOK & WORKBOOK CURRICULUM

Create Your Own Blueprint for Success

Designed for Entrepreneurs, Consultants, Career Professionals, Experts, Leaders and anyone who desires to do business in the urban market.

Order TODAY at

www.urbanmultisportconsulting.com

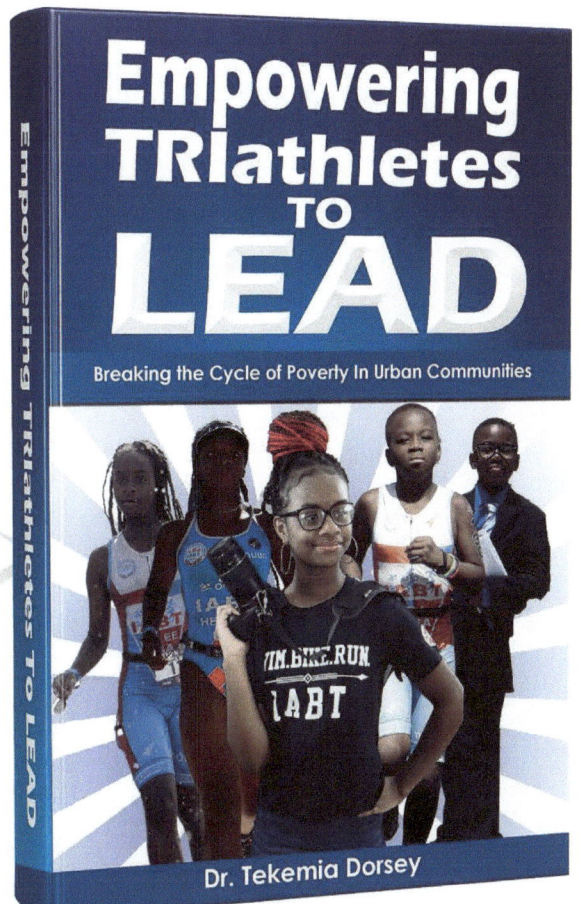 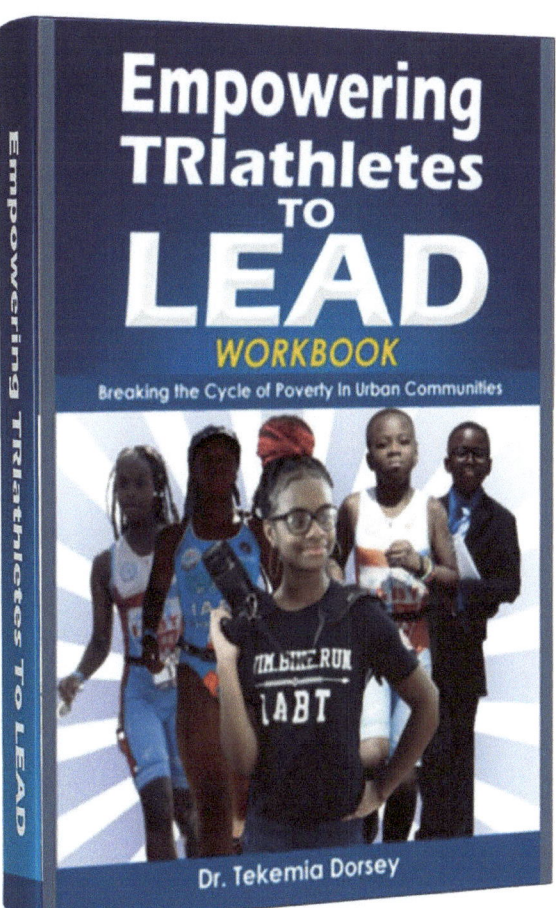

EMPOWERING TRIATHLETES TO LEAD BOOK & WORKBOOK CURRICULUM

Creating a Blueprint to Break The Cycle of Poverty

Designed for Youth Ages 10 -17 years old. A comprehensive, participant friendly curriculum to prepare youth for college and career readiness, workforce development and education, leadership training and development while, decreasing educational disparity & learning to balance health & wealth choices, plus more. Youth create a blueprint that identify current skillsets/interests that lead them to develop a strategic plan to avoid entering the cycle of poverty by the age of 18. A must have to prepare all youth, especially those living in urban communities.

A MUST HAVE TO PREPARE YOUTH TO AVOID ENTERING THE CYCLE OF POVERTY BY THE AGE OF 18.

Available in units of 50 or more

Order TODAY at

www.urbanmultisportconsulting.com

Che Brown

Che Brown is a globally renowned giant in the sales world. He has cracked the once elusive code of entrepreneurial success with a game-changing model that unlocks unlimited financial potential, power and wealth. In just six short years, he has dominated the sales space, coaching thousands of rising business leaders to achieve exponential growth and success in their industries, to the tune of over $400 million and counting. His acclaimed 7-Figure Sales Team concept has forever erased the outdated notion that generating revenue in business is a sole-source game – instead illustrating it is indeed a team sport. Che lives, breathes and sleeps his craft. He has his fingers on the pulse of profit generation and an instinctual insight into why the heart of a flailing business has stopped. Most importantly, he can resuscitate the flow of revenue in any company with just a whiteboard and a conversation. Che Brown is the CEO of EasySalesHub (www.EasySalesHub.com) scaling businesses to six and seven figures. This all-in-one solution generates leads, qualifies prospects, books appointments, closes deals and frees entrepreneurs to focus on other business needs. Che was named one of the Top 15 entrepreneurs to keep an eye out for across North America in 2021 by USA Today News. Che is the Host of the #1 Business Development and Late Night Show In The Country: The Happy Entrepreneur Show (www.HappyEntrepreneurShow.com), and Founder of Comeback Champion (www.ComebackChampionSummit.com)

www.EvergreenRevenuePlaybook.com — FREE GIFT

www.EasySalesHub.com

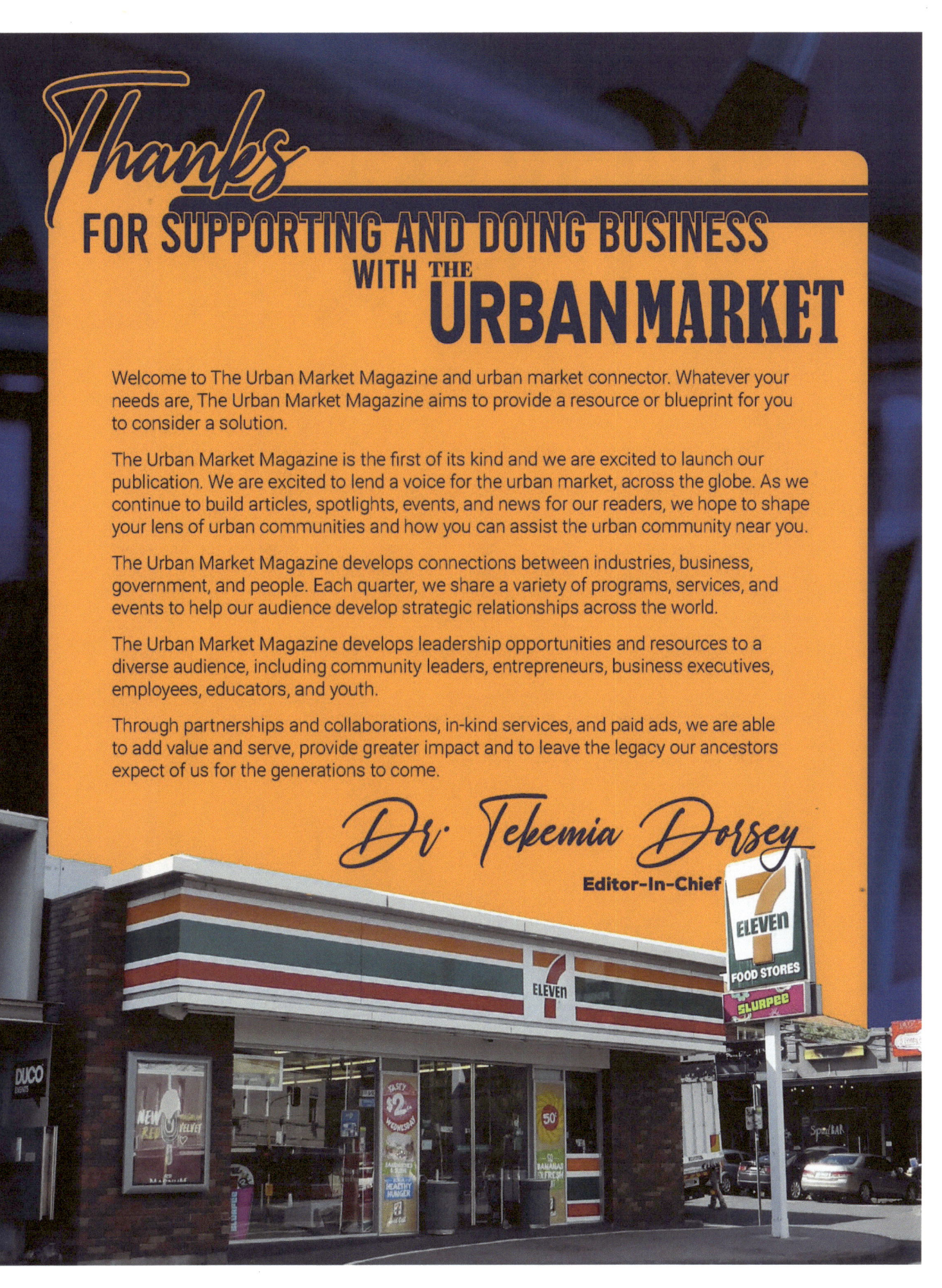

Thanks
FOR SUPPORTING AND DOING BUSINESS WITH THE URBAN MARKET

Welcome to The Urban Market Magazine and urban market connector. Whatever your needs are, The Urban Market Magazine aims to provide a resource or blueprint for you to consider a solution.

The Urban Market Magazine is the first of its kind and we are excited to launch our publication. We are excited to lend a voice for the urban market, across the globe. As we continue to build articles, spotlights, events, and news for our readers, we hope to shape your lens of urban communities and how you can assist the urban community near you.

The Urban Market Magazine develops connections between industries, business, government, and people. Each quarter, we share a variety of programs, services, and events to help our audience develop strategic relationships across the world.

The Urban Market Magazine develops leadership opportunities and resources to a diverse audience, including community leaders, entrepreneurs, business executives, employees, educators, and youth.

Through partnerships and collaborations, in-kind services, and paid ads, we are able to add value and serve, provide greater impact and to leave the legacy our ancestors expect of us for the generations to come.

Dr. Tekemia Dorsey
Editor-In-Chief

HOLISTIC HEALTH & WELLNESS

Holistic Health and Wellness LLC provides a wide range of comprehensive personalized solutions to address your individual needs. We provide evidence-based treatment for mental illness and substance use disorders. We offer a variety of services ranging from medication management to genetic testing to provide individuals with an effective client centered treatment plan. In helping you achieve optimal physical and mental health; a dedicated team of qualified professionals will work with you to design a treatment plan that meets your needs.

All of our services are provided in a calm, nurturing, and non-judgmental environment where the clients get complete privacy and confidentiality. Our aim is to not just provide mental health and medication services, but we also assist individuals in enhancing their capacity towards successful living, recapturing their integrated role in the community and society.

Battling mental illness can be extremely difficult for both the patients and their families. People experiencing a mental health condition, such as depression and bipolar are at a higher risk for suicide than the general population. Mental illness can have an impact on the overall well-being of a person, including their physical health. There are a number of medical conditions that have been linked to mental health disorders, such as heart condition, hypertension, cancer, and stroke. Here at Holistic Health and Wellness LLC we use the latest research and innovative data to provide evidence-based treatment for you or your loved ones, who may be dealing with mental health or substance use disorders.

We accept most major health insurance plan, for most services. Give us a call today to see if your plan is accepted!

Its Time To GO DEEP Summit Presents
DTDYouthX Edition
By Visionary Leaders

4X International Youth Speakers
Halee & Beloved Joshua Simons

Dr. Tekemia Dorsey
International Conference Host & Speaker

CALL FOR SPEAKERS

Our mission is to inspire youth and young adults to advocate for change by using their voices concerning issues preventing a positive transformational change in their lives and communities.

Dates: September 22-24, 2022 (International Virtual Conference [Joint Initiative w/Adamas University - School of Education])

September 24, 2022 (In person - Baltimore County, MD)

The Ultimate Hybrid Experience
www.itstimetogodeepspeaker.com

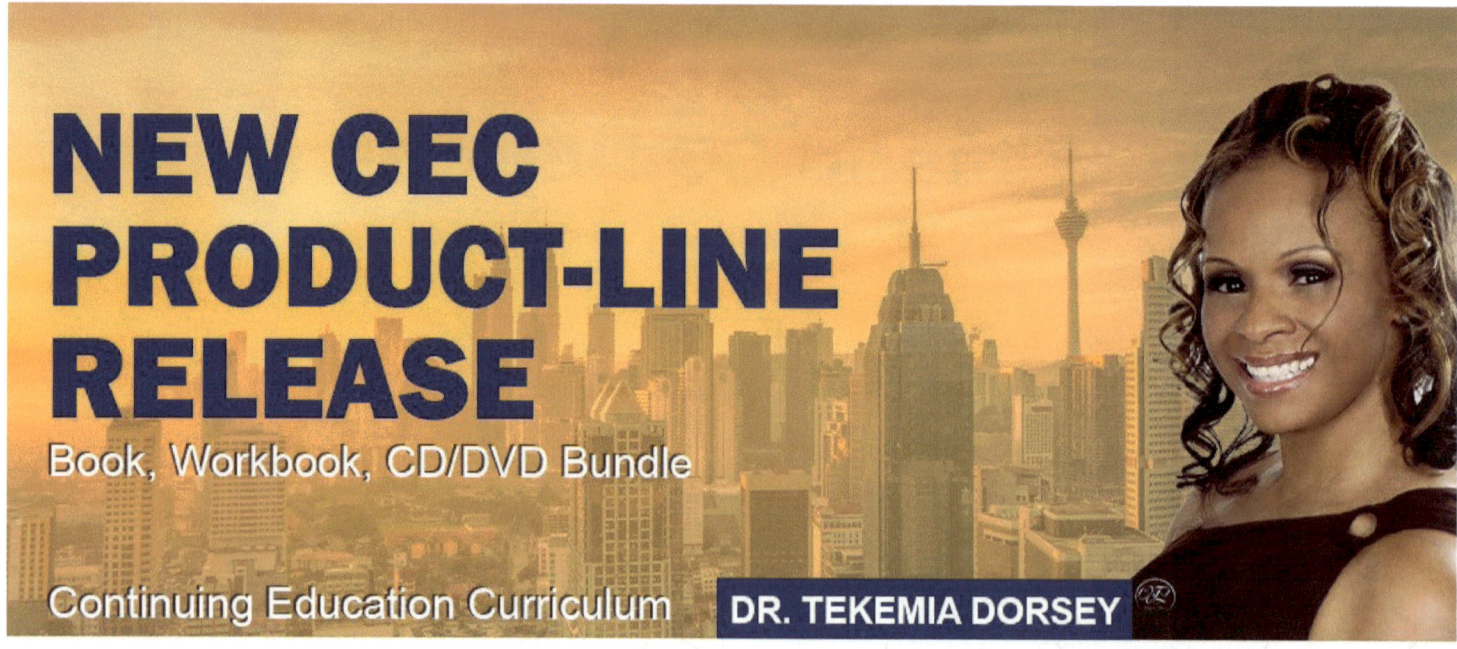

NEW CEC PRODUCT-LINE RELEASE
Book, Workbook, CD/DVD Bundle

Continuing Education Curriculum **DR. TEKEMIA DORSEY**

Our Products

 Build Your Own Blueprint While Becoming A Resource To The Urban Market BOOK

 Build Your Own Blueprint While Becoming A Resource To The Urban Market CD/DVD Bundles

 Build Your Own Blueprint While Becoming A Resource To The Urban Market WORKBOOK

 Build Your Own Blueprint While Becoming A Resource To The Urban Market Single CD/DVD

Benefits

- Adapted To All Learning Styles
- Self-Paced Program
- Creates A Blueprint That Works For You
- Evokes Action Right Away
- Meets You On Your Level Of Business
- Prepares You For Increase In Funding Opportunities
- Prepares You To Build Community Partnerships
- Prepares You To Expand Your Business Model
- Prepares You To Increase Your Finance & Revenue Streams
- Enacts The Transformational LEADER Within, Plus More

CALL TO ACTION The First 500 customers will receive a 3 Month Subscription to DTD Urban TV Network.

COUNT ME IN Receive a 10% Discount if you enroll today in DTD's School Of Urban Leadership

www.dtdschoolofurbanleadership.com

J.J. Conway

Janine "JJ" Conway was the first African American to serve as a physicist in the Air Force, where she retired as a Lieutenant Colonel after 23 years. She became a financial planner after returning from a 6-month trip to discover her house sold, divorce papers, and over $845,000 debt to her name. JJ learned how to make money work for her quickly, yet ethically. She now helps others dump debt, build wealth, and leave a legacy using the same financial management and personal growth skills. She also mirrors these principles when working with businesses to improve processes, people, and profit.

 https://www.buildingwealthtogether.com/

- f @JJKnowsTheWay
- 📷 @JJKnowsTheWay
- 🐦 @JJKnowsTheWay
- ▶ @JJKnowsTheWay

Retrieval: THE SECRET TO STUDENT SUCCESS

Learning is definitely an art, however cognitive science can help make a student's learning experience a masterpiece! Parents, regardless of their skills in math and science, are highly capable of being involved. There are three steps in the learning process: encoding, storage, and retrieval. Retrieval, the act of recalling something one has learned in order to say it, write it down, or apply it, can be a game changer for your students. Just think for example, of a recipe you might make once a year versus one you make once a month. Which one can you remember easier? The difference is the time between retrieval. Cognitive researchers have found that retrieving something on a monthly basis leads to long term retrieval of any subject, algebra included!

The easiest form for teachers and parents to use to help their scholars is a brain dump. Give a student three to five minutes to write down everything they learned about a certain subject. Then give them feedback to help them add missing information and correct errors. When students have to retrieve information, it's not simply a memory game, it helps their long term retention of material they've learned. The age-old question "What did you learn at school today?" is a good one because it's about retrieval. But, since the most common answers given are vague at best, parents could consider changing to an at-home brain dump where they insist on the details. The brain science suggests that using retrieval strategies such a brain dump to have students give more thoughtful, regular retrieval responses

can help them increase their grades by a letter or even two. Researchers found that using retrieval practices students who normally earned a C in class were able to become A students!

There are other strategies and ways of retrieving information including retrieve taking, retrieve cards, and two things, but the most important components of each one are spacing and interleaving. Spacing refers to how much time has gone by between when a student learns something and when they have to retrieve it. Giving students the opportunity to recall and practice things from a week or a month ago is a very powerful tool to develop long-term retention. To make the practice even more effective, utilize interleaving. This means combining similar concepts together that require different strategies. In a math class, for example, the student may be asked to solve two right triangle questions, where one asks for the area and the other needs a side solved by using the "Pythagorean Theorem." Giving a student practice problems from different sections of the textbook in one assignment is an easy way of doing both of these.Aut

When students are struggling we always want to put them in front of someone who can help. Parents often get a tutor, teachers invite them to come to office hours, the answer is always extra time and practice is needed. But, by empowering them with the science of learning, that may be all they need. Even more to the point, without the science of learning being applied, all that extra time spent may not be effective. In fact, we can all make sure they regularly retrieve their learning and when gaps are identified, that they self-advocate and ask questions. We can help our scholars on the path to achieving the greatness we desire for them and if they know the science of learning they'll always find their way.

Author:
Justin Field

HALZ S. ENTERPRISES
ELEVATION, INSPIRATION, LEADERSHIP

Halz S. Business Academy
Presented by Halz S. Enterprises, LLC

Halz S. Business Academy is a membership based service where we provide training (online courses), consulting, and networking for entrepreneurs, small business owners, non-profits and youth.

Our online business academy is for leaders, experts, career professionals, consultants, entrepreneurs and youth who want to enhance their personal development, while learning to increase their revenue stream and visibility in business.

SPECIAL OFFER
Annual Membership

Youth Leaders: $25.00
Individuals: $150.00

Limited to the First 100 People.

Benefits Include

Access to NEW Course Releases

NEW Digital Products

Discount from Affiliate Partners

Discount Tix To LIVE Events & Speaking Opportunities

Monthly Meetings

Networking Opportunities, and the list continues

Grab Your Spot NOW

www.halzsenterprises.com

BELOVED J. BUSINESS ACADEMY
Presented by Beloved J. Public Speaking Firm

Beloved J. Business Academy is a membership based service where we provide training (online courses), consulting, and networking for entrepreneurs, small business owners, non-profits and youth.

Our online business academy is for leaders, experts, career professionals, consultants, entrepreneurs and youth who want to increase their knowledge and skills to elevate self, leverage their products and services and scale their net-worth and business acumens.

SPECIAL OFFER
Annual Membership

Youth Leaders: $25.00
Individuals: $150.00

LIMITED TO THE FIRST 100 PEOPLE.

Benefits Include

Access to NEW Course Releases
NEW Digital Products
Discount from Affiliate Partners
Discount Tix To LIVE Events & Speaking Opportunities
Monthly Meetings
Networking Opportunities, and the list continues

Grab Your Spot NOW
www.belovedjspeaks.org

Moriah Finley
TILE CRAFTS

Hi, my name is Moriah. I'm going to tell you how to make tile crafts! These are great for gifts, or to just make them. Here is what you need two small tiles, or cardboard rectangle paper, a ruler, scissors, glue, or a glue gun, and paint (optional).

FOLLOW THESE STEPS TO MAKE TILE CRAFTS:

Get two tiles (not like the ones on the floor, but a small one where you can cut out cardboard squares or rectangles). I got these small rectangles tiles at Home Depot. When you get yours, make sure they fit together? Then take the measurements of the tiles with the ruler. Once you have that done, take the paper and draw a ruler angle of the measurements.

Next you can trace or draw a picture that fits in the rectangle. It doesn't have to be a whole picture, it could be a gift, hearts, or something else. Nonetheless, make sure that the pictures go together because the tiles need to align properly to fit together. Then when you have your picture done, cut out the picture and glue it to the tile. I used a hot glue gun. Once that's finished, you can color the pictures with paint or crayons, if you want. Then put them together, and make sure you like them. Then they are complete!

Majesty Finley
ROYALE HIGH

Hi there! I'm Majesty and we are going to be talking about Royale High on Roblox.

It was created on April 4, 2017, by Callmehbob. The Original name was Fairies and Mermaids Winx High School which you can still play today. Royal High was its Beta and first started out on November 17th. Along the way it was getting more and more popular and new developers were helping out.

Today, the game has skyrocketed with 95.2k playing and with 7.1B visits. In this game you can role play, dress up, have an adventure with friends, complete Quest on events, battle, collect badges, trade, and win hulas or trade to get one. Royale High has 12 areas you can go to. My favorites are Enchantix High Sunset Island Apartments in Royale High. They're also a daily mini quest which is computer login in apartments, Lucky Spin Wheel on Earth and, the Fountain of Dreams which you make a wish.

Diamonds are like your money that you can spend. They also have seven passes that you can buy with Robux and I have 2 of them. There is a problem with Royal High. Everything is really expensive. I recommend Looking up tips on YouTube from other popular Royal High players who know their stuff.

Callmehbob is an American Roblox game developer known for creating Royale High, a popular fantasy roleplay game. She owns the fan group Enchantix High School for Fairies and Mermaids. She is married to **Launcelot Handsome**. She often goes by the nickname "Barbie" from fans and in her social media.

Philip Wiggins

TEENPRENEURS U.N.I.T.E. TO BUILD YOUR OWN WEALTH

I'm going to share with you how you as a teen can begin to build your own wealth.

This doesn't just help you not be dependent on your mom and dad, but you can also build enough money to have lots of fun for your whole life. I want to give you 5 steps that form the word UNITE.

U – Unique Goal. It's important to have a goal that is special for you. It can't be just about making money. You need to be someone who wants to make a difference. Everyone else wants to just make money and doesn't have a unique goal. People are attracted to those who want to make a difference. When I was on TV one time because of my YouTube channel, someone came up to me in the restaurant and gave me $20. He said it was for me because I was making a difference.

N – NOW. What are all the things you can do NOW to make money. What can you do with no help? What could you do with a little help? And what could you do with a lot of help. For the ones that would need help, who would you get the help from, and is it worth it? Or would you be better to do something else you can do by yourself? Is there anything you can do NOW to make some dough? For me, I like making money in the easiest way possible. Something quick and easy with a nice reward. Something I can do anytime I want to, to make some quick money.

I – Individual. you have to be YOU. My mom kept trying to make me a scientist. I'm good at math but it's boring. I never told her though. I didn't want her to get mad. Only when I was honest about what *I* like and about what *I* want could she help me make decisions that were about ME and not HER. You have to know who you are and what makes you special because that's the only way to stand out with everyone else trying to make money. I make bets (like who can I beat at arm wrestling) but when I lived in the dc area my friend had a very popular you tube talking about shoes. Shoes wouldn't have worked for me, so I made money mowing lawns. I'm glad I live where arm wrestles and silly stunts make me money because it's easier and it's fun. But I'm also good at fixing things and painting and lawn work, so I could do those things if I really had to

T – Team get a team. It can be your mom. Or it can be someone you trust at school or work. John Maxwell says leaders aren't successful unless others want them to be. When you get others to love you and want you to succeed, they will help you. They will open doors for you and pay you sometimes more than you deserve. My mom says listen to old people they know stuff. She's usually right about this type of thing. I've had my fair share of help in the past 10 years of my life. Make sure you have the right people helping you. Older brothers are always a yes. Younger brothers are always a no. At least my younger brother. He is a controller. Make sure it's someone who loves you and not somebody who will try to control you. Or try to take advantage of you. My little brother won't try to take advantage of me, but he will try to control everything I do so he's not ready to be on my team.

E – Excellence. No matter what you do you have to do it with excellence. You have to figure out what the person who is paying you wants done and then do it just a little bit better than they expect for what they're paying you. That doesn't mean you have to be perfect or waste all your time. To be extraordinary doesn't take perfection, it just takes a little extra over the ordinary that everyone else is doing. When you do your job better than expected, you are now the person that people want to work for them, which later on helps your reputation as you keep getting better.

MATH AND READING
GROUP AND 1-1 SESSIONS

PEER TUTORS OF MARYLAND

SCHOOL YEAR PROGRAM

SCHEDULE

FREE STUDY HALL (TUES/THURSDAY)	4:00-4:30 PM

MATH GROUPS - TUESDAY & THURSDAY

1ST - 7TH GRADE GROUPS	4:30-5:30 PM
8TH - 12TH GRADE GROUPS	5:30-6:30 PM
DROP IN TIME	6:30-7:30 PM

READING GROUPS - TUESDAY & THURSDAY

8TH - 12TH GRADE GROUPS	4:30-5:30 PM
1ST - 7TH GRADE GROUPS	5:30-6:30 PM

CREATIVE WRITING - WEDNESDAY

3RD - 12TH GRADE GROUPS	5:30-6:30 PM

1-1 SESSIONS - TUES/WED/THURS

1ST - 12TH GRADE READING AND/OR MATH	4:30-8:30 PM

PRICING (TOTAL FOR SESSION)

GROUP STUDY	$125
ONCE/WEEK 1-1 (PEER TUTOR)	$225
TWICE/WEEK 1-1 (PEER TUTOR)	$425
ONCE/WEEK 1-1 (TEACHER)	$500
TWICE/WEEK 1-1 (TEACHER)	$1000

*ALL GROUP STUDY IS RUN BY A PTM TEACHER
*SIBLING DISCOUNT OF $25 PER CHILD

HOW TO SIGN UP

REGISTER NOW AT
PEERTUTORSOFMARYLAND.COM
AND LET'S ACE IT TOGETHER!

CONTACT MR. FIELD
E: FIELDJUS@GMAIL.COM
P: (586) 484-4828

Beloved Joshua Simons

THREE TIPS TO INSPIRE AFRICAN AMERICAN MALES W/A DISABILITY TO LEND THEIR VOICE FOR CHANGE

TIPS#1 BEING OPTIMISTIC ABOUT NEW THINGS.

The problem that African American youth males with a disability face are that they don't believe they can live a normal life, even with a disability.

According to the National Center for Disability and Journalism, approximately 6 million African American males in the U.S. live with a disability, and from kidsdata.org, 7.8% of those African American males are youth.

As African American youth with a disability, you can feel normal by

1. Accepting yourself for who you are and
2. Understanding that your disability doesn't define you.

In my earlier days of living with my disability, I didn't accept myself for who I was nor understood that my disability mentally didn't define me. My disability is called a neurological tic disorder. A neurological tic disorder is when your limbs and parts of your body start to lose control. You start you experience facial and vocal tics too. In 2014, I started training to compete in triathlons, consisting of three disciplines; swim, cycle, and run. In 2016, at the age of 8, my sisters and I went to West Chester, Ohio, to compete in our first Youth and Junior National Championship, in which the water portion of the event is open water, like the Atlantic Ocean. At the start of the swim, I experienced an anxiety attack for two reasons,

1. In my previous swim practices, I had experienced a loss of a limb, meaning my arm wasn't functioning like it was supposed to, and
2. I still wasn't comfortable swimming in open water.

So, I immediately hopped back out due to my anxiety attack when I hopped in. The officials guided me to my coach (my mom), where she calmed me down. She gave me a pep talk and remembered all the training that got me up to the moment in my life. Even when she did that, she gave me two options: back out and got eliminated from the race or hop back in and try again. This was a defining moment for me to accept who I was and understand that my disability doesn't define me. So, I trusted my training, hopped back in the water, and completed the race. This made me feel accomplished, inspired, and motivated to face my fears, and I kept pushing forward. As an African American young male with a disability, you will encounter scenarios where you too will have to choose the choice of the unknown or the choice of the known. The choice of the known, meaning you don't accept who you are and let your disability define you, and the choice of the known, accepting yourself for who you are and understanding that your disability doesn't define you. And if you choose the right choice, you will become optimistic about future possibilities.

TIPS#2
IDENTIFYING YOUR INTERESTS.

The problem that African American male youth living with a disability face is that they may be stuck, figuring out what they want to do in the future. They may be stuck because of not accepting who they are, not understanding that their disability doesn't define them, or that they don't have the belief that they can live a normal life.

At age 6, Ralph Braun was diagnosed with Spinal Muscular Atrophy. Spinal Muscular Atrophy is a genetic disorder characterized by weakness and wasting of muscles used for movement. Even though he has this, he became one of the most famous engineers with a disability in the U.S., manufacturing a motorized scooter, calling it the Tri-Wheeler. His interest was to be normal, being able to move and/or walk just like other people do.

Throughout his life, his interest never wavered, and in time, his interest led to his newest invention. He is the inventor of the Tri-Wheeler, which means his mobile wish came true. He is also the father of BraunAbility, which means that his interest has led to assisting the ability of other disabled persons to be mobile. As African American male youth with disabilities, keep pursuing your interests in life because you never know how you might empower someone else.

TIPS#3
EMBRACING THE CHANGE IN SELF.

The problem that African American youth males with disabilities face is that they are not confident, lack a sense of belonging, experience low self-esteem, feel unappreciated, and feel that their voices are silenced. Once African American youth males living with a disability start feeling these ways, they will soon start to experience adverse outcomes such as the possibility of a dropout in school, unemployment, etc.

According to the National Center on Disability and Journalism, African American students with disabilities have the lowest graduation rates of all other U.S. racial groups and graduate significantly lower than other African American students.

We can smash these statistics moving forward through advocacy, a shift in mindset, and actions through behavior.

You're probably wondering how I'm so confident in my ability to change their outcome. How many of you have known of the achievements of Harriet Tubman, Fannie Lou Hamer, and Mary Davidson? Well, how surprised would you be if I told you all three of those individuals had a disability? Yep, Harriet Tubman had epileptic seizures and hypersomnia. Even though she had this, she still became a known hero and helped other African Americans escape slavery. Fannie Lou Hamer had polio disease, but she still advocated for civil rights.

Despite their disabilities, through advocacy, a shift in mindset, and actions through behavior, they've still become influential and aspiring leaders for African Americans.

This topic is essential for me and others like me because what I didn't have was someone to share with me through knowledge and experience that I'm not alone and that there is a whole world of us out there. Through advocacy, leadership, vision, and innovation, my goal is to break the glass ceiling on the perception of what youth with disabilities can't do to what African American youth with disabilities can do.

I am an African American male with a disability, and I wanted to share strategies and tips with other African American youth with disabilities to

1. Let them know that they're not alone, and
2. To encourage them to lend their voices for change.

Beloved Joshua Simons

TAKING THE ORDINARY TO EXTRAORDINARY!

918-900-2019

www.xtraconsulting.com

FEATURED SERVICES

ED TRAINING MODULES
- Executive Director Training Modules
- Executive Director/CEO Coaching and Consulting

GRANT WRITING
- Grant Prospect Research
- Grant Readiness Consultation

BUSINESS PLANNING

CUSTOMER SERVICE TRAINING

PROGRAM ASSESSMENT & EVALUATION
- Program Data Collection & Analysis
- Program Innovation and Redesign
- Program Outcomes and Measurements

SPEAKING ENGAGEMENTS
- Sponsor A Podcast

SMALL BUSINESS MARKETING
- Social Media Management (Lite)
- Website Redesign

BOARD TRAINING AND DEVELOPMENT

FUNDRAISING PLAN
- Fundraising Strategizing Sessions
- Fundraising Development and Consulting
- Event Planning Consultation

DIETARY ASSESSMENT AND CONSULTATION

RESTAURANT ASSESSMENT AND CONSULTATION

STRATEGIC PLANNING

CUSTOMIZED BUSINESS AND **PROFESSIONAL SERVICES AVAILABLE**

Halee Simons

THREE TIPS TO TRANSFORM URBAN GIRLS INTO POWERFUL LEADERS

TIPS#1
KNOW WHAT YOUR GOALS ARE

According to the Glass Ceiling Theory, it is a limitation for African American women in the business world since they aren't promoted or given higher wages because of their gender or race. The myth of the Glass Ceiling theory is that it's ONLY relevant to older African American women, but in hindsight, it also impacts African American Female Youth. Despite being impacted by the glass ceiling theory, African American female youth can shatter this theory by using the S.M.A.R.T Goal Formula. The S.M.A.R.T Goal Formula is Specific, Measurable, Attainable, Relatable, and Timely. Smart Goals are broken down into Short Term and Long-Term Goals. If we can set short-term goals and achieve them, then that will give us motivation to achieve long-term goals. Let me give you an example of short-term and long-term goals.

Having the opportunity to sit on the Board of Directors of a local non-profit, this gives me the advantage of attending and networking at local Chamber of Commerce Networking events. In attendance at these events, a short-term goal I had was not to be seen as a youth but as a colleague. In an attempt to achieve this goal, the first the I had to do was dress the part. To achieve this sub-goal, I put on my business suit and heels, grabbed my business cards, and practiced my sales pitch. I practiced my sales pitch so that I would not stumble or be nervous when I walked up to other Business Owners. Going to my first Networking Event, my initial goal was to walk up to business owners,

Pic: L-R: Chairman Julian Jones, Beloved Joshua Simons, Halee Simons, Chamber President, Brent Howard

introduced myself and give them a business card. I was super nervous. As I continued to attend events, my approach changed slightly. I found myself not always having to give people my business card, I was able to just have a nice engaging conversation.

After going to 4-5 networking events, Business Owners started to remember my brother and me on a first-name basis. Short Term Goal completed. Then, when that was set in place, my long-term goal was to get my business affiliated with the local Chamber of Commerce. So, my mentor and I sat down, and we called the Chamber of Commerce President. Luckily, he knew who I was from the positive impact I had every time I went to each Networking Event. We applied and waited. Sixty days later, in July of 2021, me and my brother the 1st youth business owners in the world to have our businesses affiliated with the local and state chamber of commerce's. Long-term goal achieved. As an African American Female Youth, I am here to encourage you that we can shatter this Glass Ceiling theory by using the Smart Goal Formula and setting short-term and long-term goals.

TIPS#2 LEARNING TO OVERCOME ADVERSITY IN SELF.

As an African American Female Youth, some of the barriers we face are body positivity, Self - image, self - esteem, self - love, racism, comparing ourselves to other races, and much more. The Law of Attraction states that you will attract negative things into your life, if you think a negative thought but, if you think positive thoughts, you will attract positive things into your life.

At the age of 4, my brother was diagnosed with a neurological tick disorder. When he found this out, he felt scared, sad, worried, uneased, and more. He also started to question his self-worth, his self-love, his self-esteem, and the list continues. It wasn't until he turned to the sport of triathlons that views about self-begin to change. Since the sport of triathlon has such a diverse culture, the athletes in the sport of triathlon didn't care that he had a neurological tick disorder. They only cared about him and racing successfully. When he knew that athletes in the sport of triathlon didn't care about his neurological tic disorder, it made him feel like a normal kid. **The *Law of Attraction* states that your thoughts and emotions that you perceive will manifest into your life.** If it weren't for the athletes in the sport of triathlon making him feel accepted, he would still be stuck in a negative mindset. As an African American Female Youth, I encourage you to learn and understand the Law of Attraction and turn those negative feelings into positive ones to overcome adversity in life.

TIPS #3 EMBRACING THE CHANGE IN SELF.

The problem that most African American female youth face is the environment that they live in or used to live in. An environment can impact someone's view, prejudice, and bias. African American female youth may not grow up in an environment where they can trust or rely on someone and, as a result, they will have the mindset to only rely on themselves. The Law of Assumption states that the way to create anything you desire (your wants or needs) is to assume the feeling of your wish being fulfilled. In early 5th grade, I was uncertain of what I wanted to do because I was still trying to find myself.

Even though, I had a role model, I was torn between following my siblings, myself, or my relationship with my mentor. And then, I started to explore and listen to my intuition. Then, a year later, I got into a magnet program in the field I wanted to do, photography. That was my sixth-grade year,

and I told her the same thing and told my mentor what I wanted to do, which was photography. She said no this time because I wasn't putting in the effort. After a while, I went back to her again. This time was in the fall of my 7th-grade year. My 7th grade year was my second year of learning about photography in my magnet program, in middle school, and my mentor gave me a challenge. The challenge was to learn the camera, what it does, and learn the light. This challenge was not easy; I was stuck in some HUGE roadblocks, but I was able to overcome them.

By accepting the challenge, and trusting the process, six months later, I showcased my photography skills at the BMore Healthy Expo. As an African American female youth, this is an example of The Law of Assumption. I assumed the feeling that I desired and trusted the process in my career while, even though I didn't know exactly where I imagined being, I still worked my way to getting there. I encourage you to learn and understand the Law of Assumption, change the beliefs you hold and trust the process.

This topic of African American female youth is near and dear to my heart because I lived and still live with the daily challenges shared. My goal through platforms like this is to continue advocacy, leadership, innovation, and vision in the quest to assist others that look like me and for them to know that they are not alone. Being African American, a female and a youth do not have to mean negative things, they can and will resonate positivity and take us to new heights if we desire.

Let us be the change in our own lives and for others in our community through sharing strategies, tips, and our story as often as we can and are allowed.

 ONLINE TRAINING

PUT THE SECRETS OF THE WEALTHY TO WORK FOR YOU!

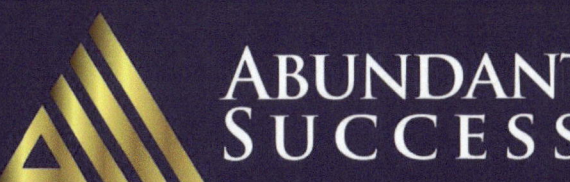 ABUNDANT SUCCESS

 INSTANT ACCESS!

28 DAYS TO FINANCIAL FREEDOM BOOTCAMP

JJ Conway

A STEP-BY-STEP BOOTCAMP TO BUILD GENERATIONAL WEALTH

LEARN HOW TO:

- BUILD WEALTH FAST
- RETIRE WITH DIGNITY
- CHOOSE INVESTMENTS
- PAY FOR KIDS COLLEGE
- DECIDE ON A BUSINESS
- TRANSFER GENERATIONAL WEALTH

ENROLL TODAY: WWW.JJCLINK.COM/28

IT'S TIME TO GO DEEP SUMMIT

#1 INTERNATIONAL DEVELOPMENT SUMMIT TRANSFORMING URBAN MARKETS

IT'S TIME TO **SUMMIT**
AN INTERNATIONAL DEVELOPMENT SUMMIT TRANSFORMING URBAN MARKETS

The *It's Time To Go DEEP Summit's* Visionary Leader, Dr. Tekemia Dorsey, designed the summit to change the *"What If...." to the "How To....."* for nonprofits, small businesses, entrepreneurs, and aspiring entrepreneurs. The Virtual Summit took place on January 13 – 15, 2022, and was filled with thought leaders, experts, coaches, and youth speakers who provided personal development and business growth training while increasing ways for attendees to become resources to the urban market.

Why was the summit so critical during these uncertain times? The summit remains critical during uncertain times of the pre- and post-pandemic because businesses are struggling and continue to do so.

By the end of 2021, 47.6% of businesses failed that launched in 2016 (Oberlo, 2021). In 2016, 733,085 businesses opened their doors. The excitement of owning a business is what many aspire in life. Opening the doors of a business is just one step in making a difference in the communities; however, it is not purchasing a business license that launches successful businesses, builds communities, or scales businesses.

Business failure can be attributed to various variables such as a lack of market research, not having a business plan, not sticking to the business plan, and lacking the ability to fund the business. Other variables include

- Not having a support team or the right support team members,
- Not pivoting the business value proposition to the right market,
- Incorrectly marketing to the desired market, and the list continues.

The most common variables that hinder growth and development in business success are the lack of opportunity for initial and ongoing personal development and business growth training to individuals and leadership inside the organizational structure.

Professional development and business training are often provided in medium and large organizations and corporations but not necessarily for small businesses, mom-and-pop shops, and solopreneurs. As a result, the disparity in business success continues to widen versus closing.

Regardless of organizational structure, success stems from leadership in positions of influence, including management.

More is needed even with resources such as Economic and Workforce Development Centers, Department of Labor, local Community Colleges, 4-year college/universities' entrepreneurship, and certificate programs.

Business failure statistics trending as of 12/31/21 were:

· By the end of 2017, 20.4% of businesses close their doors (1/5 of the population mentioned above)

· By the end of 2018, 31.2% of businesses close their doors (2nd year)

· By the end of 2019, 38.8% of businesses close their doors and

By the end of 2021, 49.7% of businesses started in 2016 were no longer in existence, leaving roughly 368,967 businesses starting January 1, 2022.

The *It's Time To GO DEEP Summit* aimed to assist individuals and leaders in their business endeavors while helping them develop a blueprint, system, process, or framework to evoke immediate action in closing the gap in taking their business or side hustle to the next level. Our summit allowed summit attendees to gain access to knowledge, workshops, and industry experts without having to spend one cent.

Our Virtual Summit met and exceeded our expectations bringing more than 30 plus speakers and more than 40 workshops in critical areas for free and providing that much-needed continuing education for individuals and business leaders in attendance.

Continuing Education Workshop topics fell under several categories:

- Personal Development
- Leadership Training & Development
- Money & Finance
- Business Development
- Gov't Contracts & Funding Sources, plus more

The *It's Time To GO DEEP Virtual* Summit was never meant to be a means to an end but a preparation and intervention resource to assist individuals to become better leaders in the business, their families, their communities, and most importantly, themselves.

There are three markets in which business is conducted in the United States. These markets are known as suburban, rural, and urban. Communities within urban markets need more resources and assistance from businesses than communities in rural and suburban markets.

In the United States, urban areas are defined by more than 1,000 people per block of area. Rural areas are the least populated areas. **Suburban areas have a larger population than rural areas***; however, urban areas have a larger population than both (Pewresearch, 2022).*

Urban communities rely on business support for solutions; however, who will step in for support if the business is struggling?

What is the difference between struggling businesses and successful ones?

- Continuing education
- Access to industry experts
- Q & A Sessions

· Being a part of a community of like-minded individuals

Dr. Sakeisha Hylick

I just wanted to take a moment and share with you what a wonderful experience I had as a part of this It's Time To GO Deep Summit. Dr. Tekemia Dorsey and her staff were amazing, just the level of professionalism organization and just you can witness, and you can feel the passion that they have for all of their speakers.

And just what was also amazing is that they included the teams, giving them as entrepreneurs, an opportunity to gain that. Spirits, that's going to help take them to the next level. So, I wholeheartedly encourage you to make sure that you are plugged into Dr. Tekemia Dorsey and everything that she's doing for entrepreneurs, and really given us an opportunity to truly go deep.

So again, Dr. Tekemia, I salute you and your staff. You did an amazing job, and I look forward to working with you again in the future.

Keever Lernise Murdaugh

My name is Rev. Coach Keever Lemise Murdaugh. I am very proud to have been a part of the ITTGD Summit as a media sponsor and keynote speaker. This summit has allowed me to do what I do best, and that is to teach, encourage, support, and promote others to step out of their own way and thrive. Dr. Tekemia Dorsey and the entire staff of ITTGD Summit were professional, engaging and thought forward. They literally thought of everything as far as having the guest appearances on Keever's Place, The Keever Murdaugh Show & Podcast strategically placed to best promote the summit. They also had plenty of speaker graphics prepared along with an outline of when to post, an easy onboarding process and links to easily submit content to prepare for the summit. They took the guess work out of everything so that as a speaker, all I had to do was focus on my talk and as a media sponsor promote the event. Thank you, Dr. Dorsey, and the ITTGD Summit team for a job well done and for having a vision, making it plain and expertly executing it. I am looking forward to next year and working closely with you all again!

Tamika Washington

By this was one of the best organized online summits I've participated in as a speaker. From the interview, to getting to know Dr. Dorsey, to opportunities to connect and grow your brand, I have to commend Dr. Dorsey and the entire team for a excellent execution of such an import tang opportunity for the urban market to grow fully in their walk as leaders, entrepreneurs and business owners. The topics carefully chosen to fit the needs of aspiring, new and established businesses were perfect and transforming give attendees cutting edge resources, strategies and experiences needed to push forward.

Marquetta Finley

My name is Marquetta Finley and I am President/CEO and Co-Founder of Xtraordinary Business Consulting LLC. I took part in the summit to serve. What I valued most about being part of the summit is the depth of transformative information and resources to help businesses and professionals aim at the mark of success. Thank you, Dr. Tekemia Dorsey, for assisting in adding value to the urban market!

Omar Abdelrehim

My name is Omar Abdelrehim and I am appreciative and grateful to be a part of the ITTGD summit. It is an honor to join in the effort to make a greater impact and serve the communities that build our country.

It is great to have such an esteemed panel of speakers and leaders that shared their knowledge and expertise with the masses.

I look forward to applying what was shared and encourage all to do the same and I am excited to see what comes next.

Til next time

Kimberly Scroggins

My name is Kimberly Scroggins, Director of Business Services for The Arc Baltimore. I participated in the Summit because most employers overlook the disability community when devising their DEI statements. The Summit provided an opportunity for me to educate the business community on the impact that employing people with disabilities can have on their businesses and encourage them to make their DEI statements an actionable item. The most valuable part of my experience as a speaker was knowing that I provided information that does not apply to just one business segment and offered solutions on how to be as inclusive as they are diverse.

Monique Grant

My name is Monique Grant of Detroit, MI and I signed up to be a part of the Summit to be impactful, provide a blueprint, be a resource and to leave a legacy! I have to say, this experience has been so amazing and rewarding! I have learned so much along this journey! I'm so thankful and grateful to Dr. Dorsey and her staff for answering the call to serve and for creating such an invaluable experience and platform for myself and the other Panelists and Speakers. Through her obedience, foresight, and vision she has shown a way to add value to the urban market and way to become a resource and solution to these problems. My biggest takeaway are the ways in which I can now inspire, lead and empower and I'm so thankful to have met and connected with such a wise and beautiful soul! Like, I told her we are forever locked in now! Thanks you so much dearie! (Cheeseface)!

SPRING COHORTS BEGIN MARCH 1, 2022
NATIONAL - (ONLINE)
LOCAL (IN-PERSON)

A community-centered, evidenced based preparation program for athletic and non-athletic students, ages 10-17 years old living in urban communities.

SIGN UP FOR AN INTEREST MEETING:
FEBRUARY 14 - 18, 2022

MUST ATTEND AN INTEREST MEETING FIRST

- Deadline for all paperwork February 28, 2022
- Parent Orientation: February 21, 2022 (6-7 pm EST)
- Student Cohort Orientation: February 22, 2022 (6-7 pm EST)

Send inquiries to
info@urbanmultisportconsulting.com

The Adamant Agency

Building Unshakeable Lives and Businesses From the Inside Out

We're a business and leadership development consulting and education firm helping you transform your business with smart strategies, better leaders and cohesive teams, and the right systems that ensure your business runs like a fine-tuned machine, even when you're on vacation.

Be a Strong CEO & Leader

Define your company's vision, design the strategic plan, and lead your team to achieve it. AND have more time to work **ON** your business, not just **IN** it, and learn to lead from your values.

Right Systems & Teams

Systems are **KEY** to business success and freedom. Having the right systems in place allows you to attract the right team for your business culture and provides the foundation they need to produce great results.

Book A Consultation Today

 757.560.1768

www.theadamantagency.com   info@theadamantagency.com

PROBLEM, PREPARATION, Progress

BY DR. TEKEMIA DORSEY

There is a lack of comprehensive, quality enriched preparation programs founded on a theoretical/conceptual framework to address the gaps needed for urban youth to succeed in life and avoid entering and overcoming the cycle of poverty.

Many youth in urban communities are unaware that their knowledge correlates to real-world experiences and academic expectations with short-term and long-term success. Familiarity is needed so that more missed opportunities are known that await them. Youth are unaware of the bleak future that awaits them before it is too late, and change is needed for the better.

Youth tend to receive the education and access to information later than required. For example, the need for students to take two years of a foreign language to apply to college is usually not shared with students in their junior or senior year of high school versus during their middle school years. Some colleges and universities require three to four years of college to be considered applicants. However, when the information is received, its overwhelming, and youth cannot understand its applicability to the real world or why they were not well-informed ahead of time.

Educational course choices vary depending on private, public, traditional, and non-traditional schooling. Each school entity has a different approach to education. Some school entities offer foreign languages and multiple languages during the middle school years. Some schools even offer foreign languages during elementary school years as well. Some elementary and middle schools offer Magnet School pathways.

Magnet schools are public schools with specialized courses or curricula in the U.S. education system. "Magnet" refers to how the schools draw students from across the normal boundaries defined by authorities (usually school boards) as school zones that feed into certain schools (Public School Review, 2019).

Magnet school course selections allow students to be introduced to the preparatory track in an area of interest before they begin high school. For example, my daughter was interested in photography in elementary school, so in the fall of her last year in elementary school (5th grade), she applied to the schools in her district that offered Communications and Journalism. When she was preparing for high school, she decided to remain interested in photography and sought out high schools that offered Communication and Journalism. Upon graduation from high school, she will be attending a four-year college/university that offers Journalism through the School of Communications as her major. From the onset of elementary school, my daughter knew what she wanted to explore as a career but, most importantly, an innate skill set she wanted to develop further. Not every school district offers magnet school options, and students must apply to magnet schools.

The Magnet School application process is designed to eliminate students who do not meet the standards and criteria set for admission. Is that fair? Fairness can be determined by whom is asked. Is that equitable? It is not equitable to those who apply and do not get in or those who may want to but did not necessarily earn the grade in their formative years. Should advanced education be available for all youth regardless of academic success? The answer is yes, but unfortunately, the education system is not set up that way.

The focus of magnet school pathways is to enhance young minds' skill sets and interests and develop them while preparing them for further opportunities in high-profile careers.

A person's range of skills or abilities is known as skill sets. Another word for skill set is interest. A person's skill set leads them down a path of success if nurtured, developed, and activated over time, whether an adult or youth.

The distinct difference with youth identifying and developing their skillsets early on is that as they grow and develop, personally and professionally, they have the opportunity to avoid entering the cycle of poverty.

Preparatory pathway programs should be available to all students regardless of their former or later academic development. Preparatory programs well-rounded in theoretical and conceptual frameworks are solutions needed in all communities, especially in communities of underserved and underrepresented populations.

"Preparation programs for youth are highly needed due to the most recent statistics and the CoVid19 Pandemic has demonstrated that having degrees and lacking skill sets for adults were not enough to decrease high unemployment rates therefore, if we do not change the focus with our youth, those living in poverty will increase sufficiently in the years to come placing youth and families in more despite conditions than CoVid19", says CEO, Dr. Tekemia Dorsey

DR. TEKEMIA DORSEY'S (DTD) SPORTS ACADEMY 4 URBAN YOUTH

Dr. Tekemia Dorsey's Sports Academy 4 is an executive leadership program for athletic and non-athletic students, ages 10-17 years old, that assists youth in developing a blueprint to break the cycle of poverty based on their innate skill sets and interests. Students learn to lead through behavior, advocacy, leadership, and civic engagement.

DTD's Sports Academy 4 Urban Youth curriculum and training are based on five core components: Leadership Training and Development, Workforce Development Education & Certification, Career and College Readiness, Health & Wellness, and a Civic Engagement Project.

WHY ARE THESE COMPONENTS IMPORTANT?

Leadership Training & Development, Workforce Development Education & Certification, Career and College Readiness, Health and Wellness, and the newly added component are essential because much is unveiled for success when a dive deep of each are explored. Students are not typically introduced to these variables all at once in a program. Suppose they become familiar with these topics later in life, such as 11th, 12th, or collegiate years. The latter years are too late to plant seeds and watch them blossom in youth. For youth in urban communities, the later years are too late to learn, explore, and capitalize on these variables for success in life.

Youth respond best through structure, time management, organization, and buy-in. Buy-in means having viable input where their voices are heard and becomes part of the process. Adults do so as well, but when youth can see the value of their experience and how it connects to the real world, they tend to take a greater interest in their personal and professional growth and development. Instead of youth sitting in the passenger or back seat of the process, they have the aptitude to become the driver of their change and tend to lead more. Youth and community leaders and partners experienced the same metamorphosis experiences through our programs.

During our 2020 Sports Academy 4 Urban Youth

IABT's Leadership, Workforce Development & STEM Hybrid Program – IMPACT

IABT Program Goals/Objectives Were Met:

- 80% of participants increased their employability skills. 80% of participants possess tools for success in college and career exploration.
- 75% of participants exited with certifications in areas that will enhance their skill sets and marketability.
- 90% of participants learned how to decrease the health disparity levels within their households.
- 90% of participants developed strategies to reduce and manage stress.
- 100% of participants learned how to become leaders in life, in workplace settings, and their communities
- 100% of our partners are now familiar with the triathlon sport, its benefit, and untapped potential for underserved and underrepresented communities.

Our 2020 Cohort of graduates met and exceeded goals set for themselves and our programming, demonstrating that youth are far more capable of what is seen through the naked eye, if given opportunities to nurture and to grow their innate skillsets and talents.

Our Class of 2020 Graduates of DTD's Sports Academy 4 Urban Youth were able to overcome one of the largest challenges faced during our programming. The roadblocks were faced during the resume exploration and creation phase of programming. By the end, they were individually and collectively able to overcome the adversity faced and with flying colors.

The Class of 2020 Cohort of DTD's Sports Academy 4 Urban Youth brainstormed, developed and successfully executed a TRIAD set of Initiatives in less than 8-weeks that benefitted the underserved and underrepresented youth, families and communities (i.e. Baltimore City, Baltimore County and Prince Georges County, MD).

TRIAD Initiatives implemented:

1. Holiday Clothes/Coat/Hat & Gloves Drive – in less than 3 ½ weeks, we were able to collect more than 1000 pieces of clothing. The pieces collected were then sorted, labeled, and bagged to give away to underserved and underrepresented families.

2. 5K Run/Walk Virtual Fundraiser – inspiring and motivating people from all walks of life to get active while fighting childhood and adult obesity for a worthy cause. Funds were raised to assist with the Health and Wellness Community Giveback Event.

3. IABT's Health & Wellness Community Giveback Event – participants adopted a local daycare center, engaged community partners for bag giveaways, and held a full day of

activity including a one-mile fun walk/run for families. More than 30 plus families were in attendance.

Each DTD's Sports Academy 4 Urban Youth Cohort graduate received an Executive Citation for County Executive, Johnny Olszewski; a from then Mayor Jack Young and then their Community Give Back Program, received honors from Governor Larry Hogan. Each participant also receiving individual honors from the State of Maryland.

DTD's Sports Academy 4 Urban Youth graduates received community service hours; became CPR/AED Adult/Child Certified, develop resumes, acquired letters of recommendations, received financial literacy training; completed college level courses, developed portfolios, and the list continues.

To Enroll a youth, nominate a youth or consider bringing our programming to your community, purchase the curriculum, email info@urbanmultisportconsulting.com or call 443-267-8783.

EXPANDING YOUTH-CENTERED OPPORTUNITIES

MEET THE 2022 ITTGD TEEN *Writer's Cohort*

We are excited to introduce a new initiative under our DTD's Sports Academy 4 Urban Youth. Tapping into the skillsets of our youth and adding more value to opportunities in the urban market. Our 2020 ITTGD Teen Writer's Cohort are dynamic youth lending their voice to change thorugh the mighty pen.

I am from Texas

This is going to be an exciting year as I elevate myself, my brand and my community as part of DTD's Sports Academy 4 Urban Youth "2022 ITTGD Teen's Writer's Cohort!"

I cannot wait to share my insights and expertise with the world from a teen's perspective. As an already International Speaker, I am extended my reach through writer which remains amazing.

I am from Maryland

As a youth with a disability, I have been able to accept who I am and what I have to offer the world thus far in life. I published my first book on 2020 and became a 4x International Speaker in 2021 - 2022.

I have come to say "YES" to experiences that will positively prepare me for the real world and as I finish my last year in middle school, being a part of the 2022 ITTGD Teen Writer's Cohort will help me become a better writer in life. A skillset all youth should have a desire to get better in.

I am from Oklahoma

Although I am in middle school, I enjoy the challenge. I am ecstatic to be part of DTD's Sports Academy 4 Urban Youth "2022 ITTGD Teen Writer's Cohort" where we aimed to LEND A VOICE to change through the mighty pen!"

I am from Maryland

I released my first book in 2020 and launched my Urban Multisport Radio/Podcast Show also in 2020. In 2021, my platform was elevated to take part in and become an International Speaker, however being a part of a Teen Writers' Cohort excites me to NEW LEVELS!

I am from Oklahoma

As I look forward to closing out my last year in middle school and starting high school in the Fall 2022, I am elated to have an opportunity through experience to enhance my skillset in writing. Writing is an integral part of life as a student, business owner and overall part of humanity. I can't wait to share with you my views of the world.

BECOME OF THE 2022 ITTGD TEEN WRITER'S COHORT (2ND QUARTER)

Complete the application form NOW and join a winning team while preparing for your future opportunities.

https://form.jotform.com/Urban_Multisport/ittgd-magazine-teen-writer-applicat

Learning the skill and power of the voice and adding value to positive change in your community. Complete the application and let's get started.

https://form.jotform.com/Urban_Multisport/ittgd-summit-teen-speaker-applicati

MODERN DAY ENTREPRENEURIAL INSPIRATION: *Halee Simons*

INFLUENCER, LEADER, AUTHOR, SPEAKER

BY BELOVED J. SIMONS

INFORMATION ABOUT HALZ S.

- **Age:** 15
- **School:** Chesapeake High School
- **Grade:** 10
- Born on May 22
- **Occupation:** Business Owner; 4x International Speaker, Best Selling and Award-Winning Author, Civic Leader, etc.
- **Main Sport:** Multisport Industry (Triathlon, Duathlon, Aquathon, etc.)
- **Business:** Halz S. Enterprises, LLC
  - **Leadership Roles:** President of the NAACP Randallstown Youth Council (Baltimore County), 1 of 2 African American Youth and only female in the world Part of a Local and State Chamber of Commerce.

HOW SHE GOT INTO THE SPORT OF TRIATHLONS

Halee got inspired to enter the triathlon sport from her mother. Her mom began competing in triathlons more than nine years ago. Her mother took her to one of her Ironman races. When she witnessed how intense and exciting the Ironman sport was, she got inspired. After the race, she asked her mother if she could do an Ironman just like this one, but Halz said she was too young. Fortunately, she was able to get into the sport of triathlons. Halz S., her older sister, and her brother began training and competing in triathlon about eight years ago.

MAKING HISTORY, ADVOCACY, AND LEADERSHIP

- Halee is 1 of 3 siblings that co-founded the IABT Junior Multisport Club in 2014.
- The club's mission is to help urban youth in underserved and underrepresented communities get more active through the sport of triathlon. There was not that much African American youth competing in triathlons.
- So, as a co-founder, she used this club to advocate, lead, and help all urban youth worldwide understand the sport of triathlon through representation, training, and competitions.

IABT JUNIOR MULTISPORT CLUB IMPACT

Using this club, she, and her siblings:

- Helped hundreds of urban youth around the globe get more active using the sport of triathlons as a resource.
- Did a 3-year campaign of helping childhood obesity.
- Sat on a worldwide board to explain why the sport of triathlons is helpful for youth across the globe.
- Hosted multiple triathlons, duathlons, and aquathons to get urban youth more active.
- Partnered with multiple businesses to spread the awareness of triathlons and the impact this sport can have on urban youth.

THE NEW NORM

BREAKING THE GLASS CEILING

Halee Simons has broken the "Glass Ceiling" theory AND changed the lives of other youth who would like to become business owners in many ways. These are just some examples:

- She is the 1st African American Youth Triathlete turned Business Owner
- In 2021, she became the FIRST FEMALE YOUTH BUSINESS OWNER in the world that became a local AND state chamber of commerce.
- She remains the ONLY African American Female youth who has grown up in the sport of triathlons from elementary to high school, engaging and competing for the last seven years on national, local, and state levels.
- She has just become the Vendor for one of the Largest Urban School Districts in Maryland.

BREAKING HISTORY

 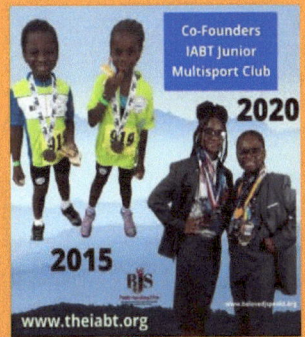

SPEAKING ENGAGEMENTS

Because of her founded business, she has been on multiple speaking engagements:

- Comeback Champion Summit 4.0
- Called2Inpire Summit (International Summit & Ambassador)
- Overcoming Childhood Obesity Through the Multidisciplined Sport Conference/Event
- IABT Youth and Junior TRI-Conference/Expo Event (Inaugural)
- IABT Youth and Junior TRI-Conference/Expo Event (2nd Annual)
- Top Teens of American Annual Prayer Breakfast
- NAACP Randallstown Youth Council (Monthly Meetings-Presiding President)
- NAACP Executive Youth Council Meetings (Monthly Meetings-Presiding President)
- USA Triathlon Coaching Education-Featured Speaker
- The It's Time To Go Deep Summit
- Building Your Wealth Summit

HONORS AND AWARDS

- Halee Simons is a member of the National Society of High School Scholars (NSHSS) for outstanding academic excellence.

- She is the 2020 recipient of several local, state and county recognitions and honors from the Mayor, County Executive, and Governor of Maryland for her unwavering advocacy, leadership, and civic engagement of behalf of underserved and underrepresented youth and communities during the covid19 pandemic.

- She is the 2019 Junior Multisport Philanthropist of the Year Award Winner.

- In 2017, her club received international recognition and honors "Volunteer of the Year Award" presented by Garmin for the work done in and on behalf of urban youth in the triathlon sport.

- She is also a 2020 graduate of DTD's Sports Academy 4 Urban Youth.

HALZ S. BUSINESS ACADEMY

Halee Simons has a business academy called Halz S. Business Academy. Her business academy launched in 2021. She made this to help others provide network training and grow to become future leaders and business owners. She also made this to acquire affiliate partners to help them to understand the youth better.

ITTGD TEEN WRITER

Halz S. is one of six youth that are a part of the ITTGD Teen Writer's Cohort. They are charged with adding their voices to change through writing about topics of interest to youth and their communities.

CHAIRMAN OF THE TEEN SPEAKER'S CAMPAIGN

Calling parents of youth ages 10-17 years old. We are inviting youth to lend their voice to change by training to hit the stage as an ITTGD TEEN SPEAKER.

Check out the minimum requirements and maximum BENEFITS!

Parents complete the application today

https://form.jotform.com/Urban_Multisport/ittgd-summit-teen-speaker-applicati

Closing the disparity gaps in literacy through the skill of speaking. Contact Youth Recruitment Committee Chair, Halz S. (Email: info@halzsenterprises.com) or Program Director, Dr. Tekemia Dorsey (Email: admin@itstimetogodeepsummit.com).

MODERN DAY ENTREPRENEURIAL IMPACT

Chamber of Commerce Networking Breakfasts

Halee is 1 of 2 youth and the only female with a business apart of the local and state chamber of commerce. Her goal was not to be seen as just youth but as a college to other business owners.

BUSINESS

- **Business Title:** Halz S. Enterprises
- **Business Birth:** February 2020
- **Mission:** "The mission of my business, Halz S. Enterprises, is to help urban youth in urban communities become future leaders in their lives."

Her business is part of the local AND state Chamber of Commerce. She has partnered with multiple businesses to help her become more financially powerful and gain more knowledge about the business world.

WHY IS HALZ S. MY MODERN-DAY ENTREPRENEURIAL INSPIRATION

Halee Simons is my Modern-Day Entrepreneurial Inspiration because she has motivated me to continue to move forward, even when things get tough. She has become a superhero in my mind (even though she gets on my nerves a bit). She is helpful in business, school, and life in general. If anyone needed advice on anything, or just someone that can listen and hear what you want to say, go to her. She is thoughtful and an extremely active person. She is funny, kind, and a hard worker. I look up to her a lot, and I love her so much

MODERN DAY ENTREPRENEURIAL INSPIRATION: *Beloved Joshua Simons*

BY HALEE SIMONS

INFORMATION ABOUT BELOVED J.

Beloved Joshua Simons is 13 years old.

He attends Middle River Middle School,

He is in 8th grade

He is a Business Owner, a Triathlete, Public Speaker, 4X International Speaker, Editor, Blogger, Podcaster, Award-Winning Author, Civic Leader, etc.

He lives daily with a neurological tic disorder.

HIS DEFINING MOMENT

BJ deals with a neurological tick disorder, and that is where parts of your limbs and body parts start to lose control, and you experience vocal and facial tics.

In 2014, BJ started to train for triathlons, consisting of 3 disciplines: Swimming, Cycling, and Running. In 2016 at the age of 8, he and his sisters went to West Chester, Ohio, to compete at their first USAT Youth and Junior Nationals.

The water portion of the event is open water; at the start of the swim, BJ experienced an anxiety attack due to 2 things: 1. In his previous training in his water portion, he lost a limb (meaning his arm wasn't functioning as it was supposed to) 2. He wasn't comfortable swimming in open water in the first place.

So, when he hopped back into the water, he immediately hopped back out due to an anxiety attack. The officials guided him to his coach; his coach calmed him down and told him to remember all the training and the hard work he had to do to get this to that point. Even when she (his coach) did that, she gave him two options:

1. Back out, quit, and get disqualified from the race

2. Go back in and try again

This scenario was a defining moment for BJ to accept who he was and understand that his disability doesn't define who he is. So, he trusted himself and his training; he hopped back into the water and finished his race. That moment in BJ's life made him feel accomplished, inspired, and motivated for him to face his fears and to encourage other youth who has disabilities like him and advocate to accept for who you are and just because you have a disability, it doesn't define you as a who human being.

active, and the IABT Junior Multisport Club became the first organization to collaborate with IABT (the International Association of Black Triathletes) to introduce triathlons to an HBCU. His club was the first to partner with six schools through Baltimore City and Baltimore County in the 2019-2020 school year, educating more than 5,000 youth in the sport of triathlons.

TRIATHLONS MAKING HIM FEEL NORMAL

LEADERSHIP

Growing up through the sport of triathlons, one thing BJ feared was not being accepted due to his neurological tick disorder. BJ thought that he would get bullied because he had a disability; he would be judged by others and not make friends. However, BJ started to realize that the youth in the sport of triathlons did not care if he had a neurological tick disorder or a disability; they only cared that he did his race and did well in the sport. This gesture by the multisport community made him feel normal, happy and he started to accept himself for who he is and feel like a normal kid.

Impact By using the club, BJ and his sisters helped hundreds of youth to get more active in the sport and used the sport of triathlons as a resource. He and his sisters started a 3-year campaign that helped get youth

- 2021 Elected 2nd Vice President of the NAACP Randallstown Youth Council of Baltimore, Maryland

- Co-Founder of the IABT Junior Multisport Club

- Serves on the IABT Board of Directors

- Scholar – Triathlete

- Maintains a 3.9 GPA engaging in all Gifted & Talented/Accelerated Courses

- He was recently elected as the President of the National Junior Honor Society (MRMS)

raises due to their gender and race. The myth only affects older women, but this is not true. It can have an impact on young females and males as well. Nevertheless, BJ has shown beyond doubt that this theory could be shattered. He is the 2nd African American Youth Triathlete turned Business Owner. In 2021, he became the First Male & Youngest Youth Business Owner to join the world's local and state chamber of commerce. He remains the ONLY African American Male youth that has grown up in the triathlon sport from elementary to now a middle school, engaging in competing for the last seven years on national, local, and state levels.

What is more exciting is that at 13 years old, he just became a Vendor for one of the LARGEST Urban School Districts in Maryland.

HONORS/AWARDS

- Beloved J is the 2020 recipient of several local, state, and county recognition and honors from the Mayor, County Executive, and Governor of Maryland for his unwavering advocacy, leadership, and civic engagement on behalf of the underserved and underrepresented youth and communities during the covid 19 pandemic.
- The 2019 Youth Multisport Philanthropist of the Year Award Winner
- In 2017, his club received international recognition and honors "Volunteer of the Year Award" presented by Garmin for the work done in and on behalf of urban youth in the triathlon sport.
- 2020 Graduate of DTD's Sports Academy 4 Urban Youth
- Has volunteer over 1500 hours in community service to underserved and underrepresented communities

BREAKING THE GLASS CEILING THEORY

What is the Glass Ceiling Theory?

The Ceiling Theory consists of women in the work field not getting prompted or getting higher pay

4X INTERNATIONAL SPEAKER

- He has spoken at the Comeback Champion Summit 4.0
- Called2inspired Summit (International Summit & Ambassador)
- Overcoming Childhood Obesity Through The Multidisciplined Sport
- IABT Youth & Junior TRI- Conference/Expo*Event (Inaugural)
- IABT Youth 8 Junior TRI- Conference/Expo*Event (2nd Annual)
- USA Triathlon Coaching Education – Featured Speaker
- Baltimore City Public School – Health & Physical Education Meeting
- Baltimore City Public School – Professional Development
- Building Your Wealth Summit
- It's Time To Go Deep Summit
- Virtual Talk w/Girls Scouts of America (Bowie Chapter)

BUSINESS ORIENTED PROJECTS

He's worked on several business projects including but not limited to The It's Time To Go Deep Summit, Halz S. Urban Multisport Radio Podcast Shows, and DTD Urban Multisport Radio Podcast Shows. He has also worked on websites, DTD's TV Network Shows, Beloved J's Urban Multisport Radio Podcast Shows, and as an independent contractor for Halz S. Enterprises, DTD's Urban Multisport Consulting Firm, and IABT.

BELOVED J. PUBLIC SPEAKING FIRM

BJ started his business in October of 2020. After learning how to grow, accept and understand his positioning and influence in his life, alongside his sisters, BJ decided to assist the population most vulnerable in the world, those living with a disability like him. Through his advocacy, leadership, civic engagement, and changed behavior, he wanted to show other young African American males with and without a disability how to use their voices for changes.

He is the youngest and only male youth business owner whose business is a part of the local AND state Chamber of Commerce worldwide. He has partnered with multiple businesses to help him become more financially robust and learn about the business world. He has met with County Executives, Councilmen Julian Jones, State Chamber of Commerce Members, and Governor Hogan's Office staff.

BUSINESS ACADEMY

His business academy launched in 2021. Beloved J launched his business academy to assist in the progression of others by providing training, opportunities to network, and a platform for current and future business owners, speakers, and leaders. She also made this to acquire affiliate partners to help them to understand the youth better.

PUBLISHED BOOKS

To help others understand the impact of the triathlon sport, as a foundation assisted in their growth and development to their rise to business owner status, BJ and his sister wrote a book that shares their backstory. They contributed to several other publications (workbook and book combinations).

The first book he Authored was Thought Leader: The Future of the Urban Multisport. The second one he co-founded was A Deep Dive: An Urban Multisport Impact Book/Workbook: This book is designed for Entrepreneurs, Leaders, Experts, Career Professionals, and Consultants. And the last book that he co-authored was Empowering Triathletes To Lead Book/Workbook. This book is a curriculum is designed for youth ages 10-18 years old to develop a blueprint to break the glass cycle of poverty in their lives.

WHY IS BELOVED J. MY MODERN-DAY ENTREPRENEURIAL INSPIRATION

Beloved Joshua Simons is my Modern-Day Entrepreneurial Inspiration because he has motivated me to continue to move forward, even when things get tough and challenging. Even though he is my little brother, I look up to him a lot because he is a person who doesn't back down and takes no for an answer. He is intelligent, friendly, hard-working, and talented. If there is anyone, I can go to for tech issues or technology people in general, I can go to BJ. He's a very athletic person and likes to be competitive in his training and school in general. I look up to him as a peer, brother, and companion.

2nd Annual
ITS TIME TO GO DEEP SUMMIT
September 22 - 24, 2022

CALL FOR PROPOSALS

REACH THE URBAN MARKET TO BUILD COMMUNITIES, LAUNCH GRASSROOTS INITIATIVES AND SCALE YOUR BUSINESS

Dr. Tekemia Dorsey
International Conference Host & Speaker

The mission of the **Its Time To GO DEEP Summit** is to provide business growth and personal development to non profits, small businesses and entrepreneurs while increasing resources to the urban market.

APPLY NOW

www.itstimetogodeepspeaker.com

A DEEP DIVE ACADEMY

PRESENTED BY DR. TEKEMIA DORSEY (DTD URBAN MULTISPORT CONSULTING FIRM)

Dr. Tekemia Dorsey's **A DEEP DIVE Academy** is designed for entrepreneurs, consultants, leaders, experts, career professionals, and those that desire to create a deeper impact in their lives, their businesses and their community. Being transformational is more than a word, it requires a changed MINDSET, changed BEHAVIOR and constant ACTION.

WHAT YOU GET

- **PILLAR ONE:** A Deep Dive Academy
- **PILLAR TWO:** A Deep Dive Mastermind
- **PILLAR THREE:** A Deep Dive TRIBE
- **PILLAR FOUR:** A Deep Dive Event

Plus BONUSES

- A Deep Dive Jumpstart Program
- A Deep Dive Roundtable
- A Deep Dive RETREAT plus more

LEARN MORE AT

www.adeepdiveacademy.com

www.ingramcontent.com/pod-product-compliance
Lightning Source LLC
Chambersburg PA
CBHW041520220426
43667CB00002B/49